REINCARNATION

WHY, WHERE & HOW WE HAVE LIVED BEFORE

by

Dr. Douglas M. Baker
B.A., M.R.C.S., L.R.C.P., F.Z.S.

ISBN 0 906006 57 0

CONTENTS

Why Should We Believe In Reincarnation?

It is surprising how many famous people subscribe to the belief that we are reborn again and again. Henry Ford said,

> "When I was a young man, like so many others, I was bewildered. I found myself asking the question, 'What are we here for?' I found no answer. Without some answer to that question, life is empty, useless."

Subsequently, he came into possession of a book on reincarnation. After reading it, Henry Ford said,

> "It changed my whole life. From emptiness and uselessness, it changed my outlook on life to purpose and meaning. I believe that we are here now and will come back again . . . of this I am sure . . . that we **are** here for a purpose and that we go on. Mind and memory — they are eternals."

Lloyd George, Prime Minister of Britain during the most vicious years of the First World War, once commented:-

> "My opinion is that we shall be reincarnated . . . and that hereafter we shall suffer or benefit in accordance with what we have done in this world. For example, the employer who sweats his work people will be condemned to be sweated himself."

Albert Schweitzer, on arriving in America for the first time, was met by a large body of people. He addressed them as follows:-

"Ladies and gentlemen, in my youth I was a stupid young man. I learned German and French, Latin and Greek, and Hebrew, but no English.

"In my next incarnation, English will be my first language."

Poets and Reincarnation

Most English children of the author's generation grew up with the poetry of John Masefield, the English poet laureate. His stirring poem *Sea Fever* expresses his thirst for life:-

> . . . I must down to the seas again, for the call of
> the running tide
> Is a wild call and a clear call that may not be
> denied . . . .

Masefield believed that the thirst for life is not expunged at the moment of death, that that thirst goes on between lives, and that we are reborn:-

> I hold that when a person dies
>   His soul returns again to earth;
> Arrayed in some new flesh disguise.
>   Another mother gives him birth.
> With sturdier limbs and brighter brain
> The old soul takes the road again.

Poets have always in the past been regarded as sages, no matter what their age. They were believed to have been visited by the muses which means, in language other than mythological, that they were divinely inspired or informed from divine levels from where, as the reincarnationists know, the mechanisms governing rebirth operate.

It is quite easy to point to a whole host of poets who, through their poetry, have indicated their love of this very ancient belief that man's soul is immortal. Certainly we should include amongst them the German poet Goethe, the English poet Tennyson, as well as William Wordsworth who describes beautifully in his *Intimations of Immortality* how the young child comes into each incarnation "trailing clouds of glory" from the heaven world:-

> Our birth is but a sleep and a forgetting :
> The soul that rises with us, our life's star,
>   Hath had elsewhere its setting,
>   And cometh from afar;
>   Not in entire forgetfulness,
>   And not in utter nakedness,
> But trailing clouds of glory do we come
>   From God, who is our home.

The American poet Walt Whitman also makes numerous references to rebirth.

Clinical Death

Amongst the author's own friends, who happen to be famous, are the late Peter Sellers and Barbara Cartland. Peter Sellers experienced clinical death in a Los Angeles hospital in 1964. Many people are having this experience in which, through a heart attack or some cerebro-vascular disorder, the blood supply to the brain is halted.

The person usually drops down dead on the street. Occasionally, if help is at hand, as it was in this particular case for Peter Sellers, the individual may be revived through modern medical techniques by applying shock to the chest wall or injecting adrenalin directly into the heart muscle and even through mouth-to-mouth resuscitation. However, until the heart beats again, the patient is clinically dead. If the period of "clinical death" is extended beyond eight minutes, the brain is usually irreversibly damaged through lack of oxygen supply to its neurons.

During this so-called condition of *clinical death*, the astral body becomes loosened from its physical frame and may even leave the physical body behind on the operating table or in the casualty station or on the street pavement, moving speedily into the astral worlds which have been its home between lives and during lives for countless millennia. Peter Sellers had such an experience which, thereafter, helped to give him an inordinate concern for the whole subject of death and the after-life.

Records of clinical death give numerous examples of people having out-of-body experience whilst the brain is suffering from oxygen deprivation (anoxia). A very descriptive example of this out-of-body experience is given by Professor Carl Jung who himself suffered clinical death in 1944.

During the period in which cardiac output had been halted and no blood, therefore, was passing to the brain, he described how he found himself high above the Earth, floating in such a position that on his left-hand side he could see the Arabian peninsula below him and on his right the subcontinent of India. Later he calculated that this must have been 1,000 miles above the Earth.

Professor Jung was a scientist of international repute, and his testimony must be accepted not only as unquestionable, but as being immaculate in its accuracy, because he was a trained scientific observer of the most abstruse matters.

Jung went on to describe how he was about to enter a temple-like structure at this level above the Earth, where he believed he would meet his friends and relatives long-since dead, when he was suddenly drawn back into his physical body. The doctors reviving him had injected adrenalin into his heart muscle, and Jung had felt this even whilst in his out-of-body condition.

Jung's description of the out-of-body state is highly relevant to our subject because the reader will want many questions answered before he is convinced of there being a credible basis to the belief in reincarnation. One will want to know, for instance, how we survive the grave, what we survive in, where we survive and, indeed, why we survive at all to be reborn. It is proposed here that the vehicle which houses our consciousness during clinical death is the same vehicle which houses it after true death, as well as when we leave the physical body in the sleep state and travel in the astral world.

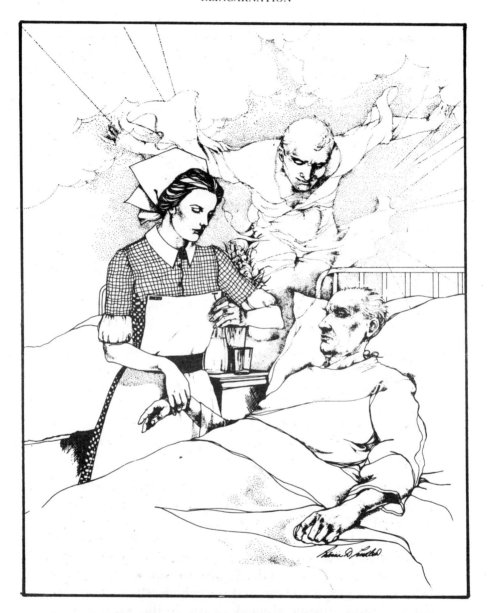

Clinical Death and Out-of-Body Experience

In clinical death, cardiac output is halted; the brain is deprived of oxygen
and the inner bodies slide out of alignment with the physical body. Out-
of-body experience may then occur. In such a state, Jung found himself
a thousand miles above the earth.

Belief In Rebirth

In 1959, a poll held in Great Britain showed that 12% of the English-speaking peoples believed in reincarnation. Twenty years later, this figure had grown to 28% when a poll was again held in 1979 posing questions about belief in immortality and rebirth. These figures are somewhat below the level of English-speaking peoples in the U.S.A. and Canada.

The author believes that by the end of the century, 50% of the English-speaking peoples everywhere will have accepted the proposition of rebirth. It forms part of his work to lecture extensively on this subject in an endeavour to change the climate of thinking on matters esoteric.

Speculative or not, we have to accept the plain truth : *more than half the world's population accepts belief in rebirth.* The numbers are, of course, much higher in the orient than they are in the occident at this time.

* * * * *

For all the scientific research, for all the vast sums spent on our educational institutes, there remain five great questions unanswered . . . questions which have plagued man down through the centuries :-

Who are we?

Where do we come from?

Where do we go to from here?

Why are we here at all?

Why do we have to suffer pain?

Passing through four universities, both in England and abroad, the author never encountered in any of them any teaching which faintly suggested answers to what must surely be basic questions.

Whilst they remain unsettled, man can hardly evolve a philosophy of life sufficient to meet the mounting demands placed on him by the stress of living today.

*   *   *   *   *

The common belief is that the teachings about man possessing a soul started with the Christian Church. It did nothing of the sort. Six hundred years before Christianity, Socrates and Plato both spoke of the existence of the soul and the long journey it has to take in its struggle towards Truth, Beauty and Goodness.

The very nature of the soul, as taught by them and by Pythagoras before them, demands the acceptance of the concept of reincarnation, for in that long journey to perfection, the soul requires many lives on earth to achieve its goal.

This immortal fragment of ourselves, the soul, was referred to in ancient Greece as the *psyche*, which is also the word for butterfly. Yet today, psychology, which purports to be a study of the psyche and its behaviour at all levels, is a pale shadow of what it should be. As Eric Fromm remarks, "Psychology became a science lacking in its main subject matter, the soul." It has retained the *ology* and forgotten the *psyche*.

We also speak of psychiatrist, which is made from the two Greek words *psyche* (the soul) and *iatros* (doctor). Who today would suggest for one moment that the average psychiatrist takes into account anything pertaining to man's immortal Self, his soul?

In the year 553 A.D., the Fifth Ecumenical Council of the church anathematised the teachings on reincarnation. The concept of the soul and the proposition that it needed many lives on earth were both examined by the Church Fathers, and the outcome was that the idea of the soul was accepted as valid, but the proposition that it reincarnated again and again was considered dangerous and accordingly anathematised.

As a result, the whole concept of the soul became unstable. It was no longer supported by the philosophy of rebirth, and today the truth is that, for most people, the existence of the human soul is no longer a reality. Instead, everywhere in the West, there is an egotism that stops abruptly only with the last breath.

The Temple at Delphi

**"Man, know thyself, and thou wilt know
the universe and the Gods!"**

. . . *From Whose Bourne*
No Traveller Ever Returns

Christianity has done her work well. She has preached the existence of heaven so that everyone wants to go there, but nobody wants to die. Rather, everywhere there is a massive fear of death. People are like ostriches: they fear death and hide themselves from it, not even considering discussion of it.

Contradiction stamps both the arrival of man on Earth and his departure from the planet. We hear nonsense about being "born into sin" on the one hand, thus the suggestion that we have committed a crime merely by being born, and on the other hand we hear of "death", "hell" and "pergatory" associated with our leaving the planet. Millions live by this nonsense or are intimidated by it to such an extent that the subject of death — really the most relevant and influential one in all the world — is spurned and vilified.

Finally, there is that nonsense taught about the resurrection: about people getting up out of their graves in their physical bodies at the sound of a host of etherial trumpets and marching off towards salvation.

*   *   *   *   *

We are all going on a journey. It is a long one. John Richardson (Shakespeare) referred to death as "the undiscovered country from whose bourne no traveller ever returns." Let us take this analogy further.

Let us suggest that you are about to undertake a visit to Outer Mongolia in three months time. What would you do about it? What preparations would you undertake?

Naturally, you would enquire whether your passport needed a visa to enter Mongolia; you would want to know whether you should establish a letter of credit there; what currency restrictions existed; whether there were suitable hotels; you might even decide to take along a little Ty-Phoo tea along with you just in case. Simply, you would take the natural precautions and steps to make your journey safe and comfortable.

Well, we are all going on such a journey, but much further and more certain. Yet, what do we find? We make no effort to understand what sort of laws might govern us in that new country, which we call death. We do not bother to find out what kind of requirements are demanded of us as we cross into that state. We pretend that its not going to happen and hide our heads from it.

Why, Where, How & When?

To answer the questions that arise immediately in the minds of those who delve into the subject of reincarnation, it is necessary here to present a resumé or thumbnail sketch of common factors extracted from a wide range of teachings from many ancient cultures which will indicate to us how we cross that frontier into the unknown, what laws govern us there, how long we stay there, what state of consciousness we exist in there, and how and when we are drawn back into incarnation.

The answers to these questions were taught in the mystery schools of ancient Egypt — where every single one of us, at some time or the other, had several lives.

We need to look into the mysteries of Greece and Rome and, long before these, into the mythologies of India and even into the Tibetan *Book Of The Dead*.

Drawing upon these ancient teachings and using symbols and images where appropriate, this is what we find :-

It is taught that life is eternal and that there is no death, only changes of state.

When I was a boy, I grew up in South Africa, a land infested with many kinds of snakes. I grew to understand this reptile and its strange expressions, and soon became aware that in these ancient teachings it was the symbol of the snake that was more used than any other. It is found throughout the Old Testament : it was the sacred occupant of temples of healing during the age of the Aesculapiads of Greece and Asia Minor : it symbolised the etheric tracts on the spine in Hindu mythology, as well as the Rounds and Races of Esoteric Buddhism.

16

The snake holding onto the tip of its tail — the uroborous — is the symbol of immortality, of life eternal. But there is another meaning that emerges in the symbol of the snake.

The snake discards its skin each year. It must do this because it grows too large for its old skin. Crawling out of the wet grass in mid-summer, it lies in an open space bathing itself in the sun's rays and then it gently sheds its outer skin, for beneath there is a newly-prepared one, larger and more adapted to the snake's form.

As a boy walking across the veldt, I often trod barefooted on the snake skins, and it was an eerie sensation. It reminded me, however, of something that I had learned at the age of fourteen when, through a vision, I became certain that my mother had survived death (her life having ended in terminal cancer).

The symbol of the snake shows that man, like the snake, discards his outer physical body again and again and continues his existence in the underlying, well-prepared "inner" skins.

Death is an illusion. Life is a continuous and unending spiral that, if anything, mounts upwards towards a continuity and perfection of consciousness which Plato said incorporated Truth, Beauty and Goodness.

What Is Man's Body?

The ancient teachings, culled from all great cultures, and the esoteric sciences show that man's physical body is only the outer skin of a more resplendent creature beneath.

The Etheric Body

Interpenetrating the physical body is a much subtler structure made of subatomic particles, described in the teachings of Theosophists, Rosicrucians, Yogis and the mystery schools.

This *etheric* counterpart of man's physical body acts as a physiological unit. Indeed, it is asserted that it acts as a matrix to the development of the physical body. The Yogis — who not only teach a philosophy based on its existence, but demonstrate the part played by this etheric body in man's totality — maintain that it is the vehicle which vitalises man's physical organs.

They have shown that when we breathe, we inhale with our oxygen the energy known as *prana*. Prana is stored in vitality globules found in the sunlit atmosphere, taken in through the respiratory system. These globules breakdown inside the etheric body and transfer their energy of prana to fine, wire-like, scintillating threads called *nadis*, which in turn channel the energy into force centres or energy reservoirs called *chakras*. It is through the control of these chakras and nadis that the Yogis demonstrate their powers of controlling the physical body with their minds.

The whole of the etheric structure is coordinated by three snake-like tracts that pass up the site of the human spine. Spiritual development is a long process in which energies are progressively drawn into chakras that open their petals

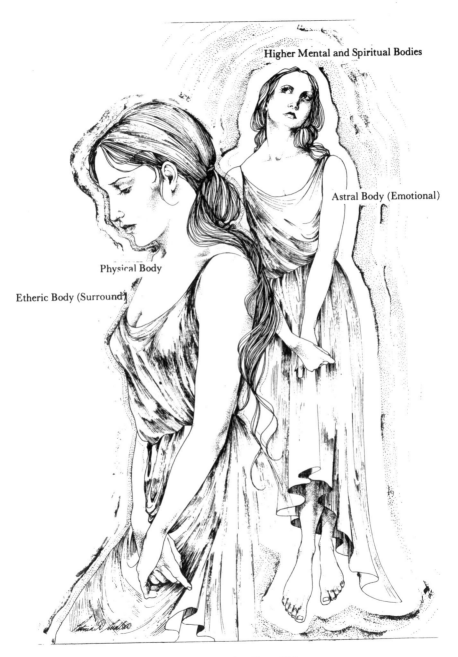

Higher Mental and Spiritual Bodies

Astral Body (Emotional)

Physical Body

Etheric Body (Surround)

The Interpenetrating Aura/Bodies of Man

in a coordinated manner, reaching from the Base of the Spine to a thousand petalled lotus/chakra in the Head.

No living thing is without this etheric body, and all living things live in a continuum of etheric substance which was referred to in ancient days as the *anima mundi* of the Earth.

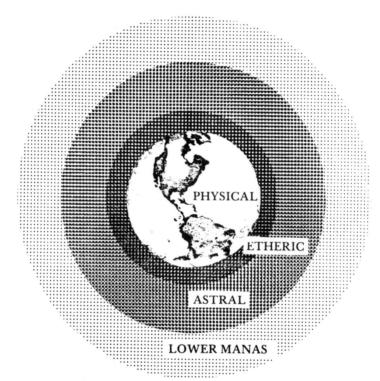

**The Composite Earth
With Interpenetrating Planes**

The Astral Body

The matter does not end here. There are even subtler states of matter which are beyond the physical. There is emotional substance called *astral*. Indeed, there is an astral globe inter-penetrating our planet and extending for a distance of about 2,000 miles beyond its surface into outer space, almost as far as the Moon.

This *astral globe* is several billion years older than our physical world. Indeed, the Earth, as we know it, derived from the nebula dust of our Solar System which was precipitated into this astral vortex. Man existed in an astral sheath in this astral world billions of years before he materialised a physical body.

It is hard for the Westerner to conceive of mental and emotional substance, and yet, most people accept that there is a spiritual essence. The proposition here is that there are subtle states of matter ranging from the gross, physical material of solid, liquid and gas right through etheric states, astral states and mental matter, up to the spiritual, and man has a vehicle or body of expression on each one of these planes.

Just as water penetrates sand in a handful of mud and, as we know, the water in its turn is interpenetrated with gaseous air, so too are the gas, liquid and solid states of matter interpenetrated by subtler states of matter. Using this analogy then, we can see that the astral body interpenetrates the etherico-physical and radiates its energies out.

The astral world is made of emotional substance, and when any man or creature feels, he creates substance of an astral denseness in the astral world. Thus, the astral world is made up of astral or *feeling matter* of various orders or subplanes. The substance of the lowest astral subplanes corresponds to the low and negative vibrations of feelings, *e.g.*, horror, fear, hate, anguish, lust, etc.

Similarly, the highest subplanes of the astral world can be identified with the Heaven of the Christians, the Devachan of the Buddhists, the Valhalla of the Norsemen, the Summerlands of the Red Indian, etc.

The Mental Body

The last of man's personality bodies is the subtlest, and this is his mental body. We have been photographing thought for more than eighty years in Japanese universities, and manifestations of thought were photographed in the 1950's at the Delawarr Laboratories in Oxford.

In 1913 at Kohyasaan University in Japan, a powerful mind concentrated for a minute and a half on a letter of the Japanese alphabet. Twenty-five feet away in a separate room, securely wrapped and sealed in a light-proof package, the sensitive surface of a photographic plate underwent a chemical change. The man's thought substance had been photographed.

My friend Dr. Jules Eisenbud examined the thought processes of a man named Ted Serios, who had the ability to direct his thought images into a camera and to precipitate them onto senstitive plates there, even though the lens of the camera had been removed.*

* Records of these investigations can be examined in the book entitled *The World of Ted Serios* by Dr. Jule Eisenbud, M.D. (Pocket Books, New York, 1968).

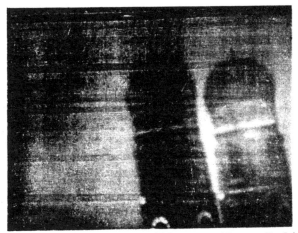

Fig. 115 (Courtesy Dr. Jule Eisenbud)

Fig. 116

Figure 115 is a photograph produced as a result of Ted Serios' mental image of the towers of Munich's Frauenkirche (or Ladies' Church) as depicted in Figure 116 (courtesy Monkmeyer Press, New York).

Man's mental body produces thoughtforms constantly. It is also capable of transmitting a fragment of its nature, perhaps a unit of energy, from one mind to another in the phenomenon of telepathy.

The Aura

Together these interpenetrating vehicles of human consciousness create an effluence which we call the human aura. The aura manifests itself in layers in the shape of an ovoid, with a mental layer on the outside, the astral layer between and the etheric layer innermost.

The American Red Indian is said to have been the most psychic race the world has ever known. The Red Indian chief was also an initiate into this esoteric knowledge. He knew of the interpenetrating subtle vehicles and their integration as the total personality of man. They depicted the layers of the aura in the headdress of feathers that they wore from head to foot.

But man's consciousness is not limited merely to these personality vehicles. They are non-enduring and are progressively cast off at death. Man possesses a soul.

What Is Man's Soul?

The soul of man is a unit of energy which is immortal and enduring. It contains the spiritual essences of Atma, Buddhi and Manas. It is the repository of those essences of spiritual experience gained from all his lives on Earth. The soul is formless and yet has been likened unto a giant lotus in the process of opening its three tiers of petals.

The so-called "young" soul is bud-like, and with each life on Earth its petals are stirred further into open expression. The sacred nature of the lotus flower was recognised in their use in the temples of ancient Greece and Egypt, as well as in India and China. The spiritual endurance of any particular lifetime produces growth in this lotus.

A thread of golden energy connects the soul — often symbolised as an upright triangle because of its triplicity of qualities (Atma, Buddhi and Manas) — to its particular personality vehicles. There passes down this thread or *sutratma* a flow of spiritual energy which constantly imparts meaning to the personality engaged in physical incarnation.

In the science of meditation, this sutratma is converted to a channel so that there is intercourse between soul and personality. A dialogue is established between the lower self and the higher. The soul rewards its aspiring personality with deluges of spiritual energy that pass down this channel — sometimes called the *rainbow bridge* or the *antakarana* — and flood the aura through its established chakras, mainly those in the Head and the Heart.

*   *   *   *   *

Some features of the soul and its vehicles are ineffable, and others may be expressed descriptively or in diagram.

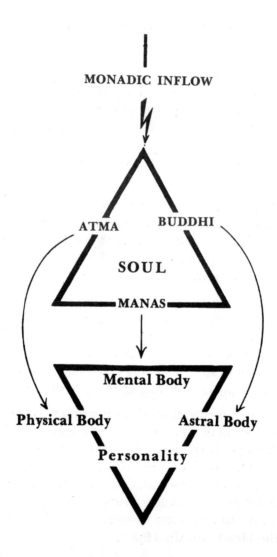

The Soul in its higher triad and the personality with its lower triad.

Many say that the soul expresses itself through our innermost natures. As Robert Browning, the English Master, wrote as a young man in his poem *Paracelsus* :-

> Truth is within ourselves; it takes no rise
> From outward things, whate'er you may believe.
>
> There is an inmost centre in us all,
> Where truth abides in fulness; and around,
> Wall upon wall, the gross flesh hems it in,
> This perfect, clear perception — which is truth.
>
> A baffling and perverting carnal mesh
> Binds it, and makes all error : and to know,
> Rather consists in opening out a way
> Whence the imprisoned splendor may escape,
> Than in effecting entry for a light
> Supposed to be without.

Where is the evidence for these basic tenets of Ancient Wisdom?

The scope of this book does not lend to detailed information about recent developments in photography which go some way to corroborating the existence of these metaphysical observations, nor to the discoveries of Dr. Walter Kilner who sensitised the human eye with dycianine screens so that it could observe the interpenetrating force fields of the mental, astral and etheric bodies. Instead, the author has decided that the testimony of the Yogis is more pertinent at this time.

Yogi Astounds The Medical World

Britain has had four hundred years in association with India and has become blasé about the feats of yoga. Yet, it is through this sacred science that the teachings of Ancient Wisdom are best expressed and demonstrated.

In the early 1970's, my great friend Swami Rama, probably the best known Yogi in the world today, was staying with me in my home. He was on the way to North America and showed me a list of various physiological feats that he was about to undertake for the Menninger Medical Foundation at Topeka, Kansas, U.S.A. It was quite staggering. He was proposing to offer himself as a "guinea-pig" for investigation under scientific test conditions of various feats of body control, some of which I had already witnessed earlier.

His journey to North America is now part of medical history. The feats that he demonstrated at the Menninger Foundation have been even responsible for the emergence of a completely new medicine, known as *biofeedback*. Young people going to medical school today will study textbooks in which Rama's astounding feats are recorded.

The following are some of the things that he was able to demonstrate under test conditions, sometimes before whole groups of doctors :-

He was able to raise the temperature of one part of his body to a much higher level than other parts, when we all know that man is homoiothermic and keeps an even temperature at 98.4°F. The author himself remembers Swami Rama demonstrating on one occasion his ability to make one leg as cold and icy as that of a corpse, whilst the other was red and hot with engorged blood.

28

Swami Rama was able to raise and lower his blood pressure at will, and from these procedures there has developed psychological techniques monitored by instruments which enable sufferers from high blood pressure to observe which of their behavioural patterns are responsible for raising or lowering it. Through subsequent intervention, using this biofeedback method, individuals can raise or lower their levels accordingly — the advantage of this new kind of medicine being that drugs used in hypertension can be dispensed with.

The phenomenon of controlling the rate of the heartbeat has always fascinated man, and Swami Rama demonstrated his ability to stop cardiac output, presumably by inducing fibrillation. By various acts of sustained will-power, combined with breath control, all monitored by an electrocardiogram, this extraordinary Yogi altered the output of blood from the heart, thus depriving the brain of oxygen for a sustained period (about six minutes or more). *What he was virtually enacting was the condition of clinical death, to order!*

So impressed were the laboratory assistants monitoring his heart waves in the adjoining room by the condition of virtual heart "arrest" that they rushed in with resuscitation equipment to bring the Swami back to consciousness and to abort clinical death. They found him, however, fully conscious and calmly talking to the investigating professors of neurophysiology. *At will, he could restore heart function.*

Under other conditions, he was able to put himself into deep coma and yet was able to remember questions put to him in this state which would normally spell complete unconsciousness to the average individual.

When the organizers of these various experiments asked His Holiness what anatomical tracts he acted upon to produce the phenomena described — that is, which brain tracts, blood vessels and nerves were involved and susceptible presumably to the actions of his mind — the Swami calmly told them that the parts he controlled in the phenomena were not yet described in Western anatomical works. He was referring, of course, to the chakras, nadis and tracts of Ida, Pingala and Shushumna which exist in the *etheric* part of man's physical nature.

It is for this reason that the author mentions Swami Rama's phenomena, namely, to show that whilst the evidence for the existence of these structures is slow in forthcoming, their functional capacities are well known for the phenomena they have produced in physical structures demonstrated in India and now in the West frequently.

The mechanics by which we reincarnate are illustrated in our diagram opposite :-

1. The soul on its own plane, feeling the urge of the "Will-to-Be" once more, puts part of itself down into the mental plane.

2. In the mental plane the soul vibrates the mental permanent unit, permanently ensconced there during and between lives, which then attracts towards it mental atoms of a similar vibratory rate that then form a mental sheath.

3. Within the mental sheath, the soul then activates on the astral plane the astral permenant unit and, in the same way, formulates the astral sheath.

4. The sheaths now hover over a fertilised human egg, pre-selected by the soul. Progressively, the embryo and the foetus are occupied, especially during the period of quickening when the limb buds suddenly grow extensively.

5. As the child matures into the adult, the soul has ample opportunity to secure its increasing hold on the physical body. This will be affected greatly by the extent of the spiritual orientation of the assumed personality.

6. The personality expresses to some extent the purpose of the soul, wears out its physical body and discards it at the end of the incarnation.

7. The consciousness after death loses the rationalising faculties of the physical plane and its etheric counterpart, but life goes on in the astro-mental body formed out of the astro-mental sheath during the incarnation.

8. The astral body has been discarded and consciousness has continued on the mental plane in the mental body which is now discarded in what is called the "second death".

9. The passage through the astral plane and the mental plane takes about fifty years. Life in the astro-mental body continues for about 20-25 years but after that, the astral shell is discarded. There is a further period of life in the mental body of twenty-five years.

10. The *second death* occurs. The last vestige of form is discarded, this being the mental shell.

(Continued bottom of page 31.)

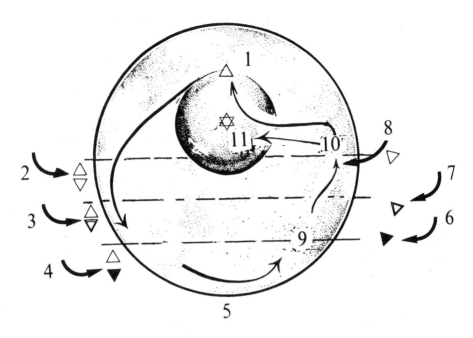

KEY TO THE GLYPHS :-

△ The Soul
✡ The Soul overshadowing
▽ The Mental Sheath
▼ The Astro-Mental Sheath
▼ The Physical Body

▷ The Mental Body (discarded)
▶ The Astro-Mental Body (discarded)
▶ The Physical (corpse)

THE SOUL'S JOURNEY
(Cyclo-spiritual Metamorphosis)

11. The remaining consciousness is spiritual, comprising those experiences conforming to Atma, Buddhi and Manas manifested in the life just vacated on Earth. These, as a unit of energy, enter the heaven-state where the soul overshadows them, abstracts the elements of Atma, Buddhi and Manas to the extent that nothing eventually remains of the last personality. The soul remains in the heaven world until the Will-to-Be reasserts itself and the cycle of rebirth begins again.

* * *

So much for the theoretical side of our subject. Impressive though the traditional teachings are, we need to have some personal verifications of its expression.

For me, reincarnation explains the apparent injustices of life. Testifying for my own generation, which lived through a World War and had more than its fair share of pain and suffering, it often seemed to many of us that there were those who appeared to escape what the Church has called "the wrath of God", who seemed always to escape sorrow and suffering without any worthy reasons.

However, through a belief in reincarnation, the author quickly realised that everything in life is compensated for. No one ever escapes. Sooner or later, in this life or in another, matters are evenly balanced. No one passes through his hundreds of lives on Earth to emerge more scarred than another.

Let us take two examples of apparent injustices and compare them :-

> A soul is born into the body of a little girl who, from the moment of birth, seems to be in constant pain. It is soon discovered that she is suffering from cancer of the bowel. She lives for five years, never knowing a day without suffering and finally expires in the arms of her horrified family.

Compare that life with the following :-

> A soul incarnates in the body of a little boy, born into a wealthy family with position and rank. The child grows up in happy circumstances surrounded by a loving family, is well educated, gains position in the world, is lithesome of form and handsome of feature, marries well, has a large family and

lives on to eighty years of age in happiness and contentment.

When we compare these two in the light of, say, the Christian teachings — namely, that we have only one life on Earth — surely it seems the height of injustice that the little girl's only experience of life on our planet is one of confinement and daily sessions of pain, so that that life stands out almost in caricature when compared to the life of the little boy growing up in affluence and happiness and living on into old age. Yet, the doctrine of reincarnation explains these apparent injustices.

The reincarnationists would point out that the little girl has had many lives on Earth previously, in which she would have lived on into old age with large families, having had every opportunity to enjoy the blessings and happiness which Earth has to bestow on occasions. Similarly, the little boy has known early death, has died in great pain from some mortal wound and has known isolation and despair, as well as those features of the life described above.

Everything is compensated for so long as we take into account that there have been other lives, previously lived and still more lives to come, in which apparent injustices are reconciled.

Then there is the matter of genius.

What Is Genius?

Genius has never been explained scientifically and, to the author's mind, not even by any department of philosophy or psychology. No one can say in terms of atoms and molecules, in terms of light, heat and magnetism, what mechanisms are at play in the production of a genius. Not even heredity offers a satisfactory explanation.

We only know that in a small percentage of the population, there suddenly emerges in the most unexpected locations a genius. It is rare for the average person not to come across one sooner or later in the normal course of events.

Mozart provides an outstanding example of the phenomena which genius presents :-

> Born with absolute pitch, infallible rhythm and natural comprehension of harmony, at the age of four he began to learn to play the clavier (a fore-runner of the modern piano) and at five picked up a violin and, reading at sight, staggered through six trios with his father and a friend. As a child he read and wrote music before he could do as well with his A-B-C's. At fifteen, he was the author of fourteen symphonies and six short operas.

There is no explanation for the genius of a Mozart or for that of a more versatile genius like Winston Churchill in terms of orthodox thinking. There is, however, a very good explanation for it once the mechanisms of rebirth are understood.

In the case of Mozart, we know that his two previous lives were as musicians, and that the period between his life as Mozart and the one immediately preceding was less than twenty years (this being one of the many exceptions to the average period between lives of about 1,000 years). The boy was able to retain memories of his musical faculties and carry them over into his current life.

How else could you explain such matters as genius?

There is one other explanation feasible: that of overshadow-ing, where a musician is retained in the astral world beyond the normal period of occupation and is able to impress or *overshadow* a suitable individual already incarnated. However, that is another matter altogether.

KARMA
The Law Underlying Reincarnation

By now the reader should be impressed by the collective evidence supporting the idea of reincarnation and would be hardly surprised to discover that certain great laws thread their way through the whole fabric of rebirth.

Science accepts that Laws govern the universe. There are laws that govern water and the flow of sap in the trees; there are laws that govern the planets in their orbits; laws that decide the pressure of the blood, the rising of the tides, the setting of the sun. There are laws for every kingdom of Nature and for every aspect of Life. Surely then, there must be laws for the times and ways in which Man must be born on Earth and for when he dies. Why should birth and death be exempt from Law, when all else is governed by it?

The Law of Karma is part of the ancient teachings. The idea that in past lives we sow the seeds of disaster or success for our present life is very old. We need only refer to the Old Testament teaching :-

> "Whatever a man soweth,
> That shall he also reap."

There emerges the idea of retribution, that if we commit some travesty of the laws of nature, then the responsibility that we owe to the Human Kingdom becomes manifest: we must suffer accordingly.

If, in some previous life, we cruelly blind a person, then we ourselves must suffer in kind. Thus, whether in that particular life or in some life ahead, we too will be blinded under cruel conditions. This may be accomplished either in a single event, or we might suffer from diseases of the eye

35

perhaps in a dusty country like Egypt somewhere in the future, even over a series of lives, but retribution is assured.

Equally so, our good karma too reflects in lives ahead.

The great Law of Karma is linked to the laws that govern reincarnation, as is demonstrated by the words of Buddha :-

> "Who toiled as a slave may come
> anew a prince, for gentle wor-
> thiness and merit won.
>
> "Who ruled as a king may wander
> the Earth in rags for things done
> and undone."

Karma and reincarnation explain why some men survive a war when other seemingly "better men" do not . . . why a child of four should die in extreme pain when others live happily into old age.

The action of karma is nicely demonstrated when we take life as a sine wave, an oscillation between positive spirit and negative matter, with consciousness forming the wave pattern. Man is on a journey which takes him out of the heaven world of spirit progressively down through the planes into material form. Life in the physical body is represented by the lowest thrusts of the life wave into material conditions. (See diagram.)

We understand then that karma will out. In the great swing of the karmic pendulum, effect follows cause. The pendulum swings back to its resting point and passes on into its next effect.

People have variable loads of karma to carry. Where karma is very heavy and very physical, it may work out as accident-proneness. For almost inexplicable reasons, certain individuals seem to be involved in accident after accident and in unending episodes of violence.

In a horoscope where Mars is afflicted to Uranus or in con-

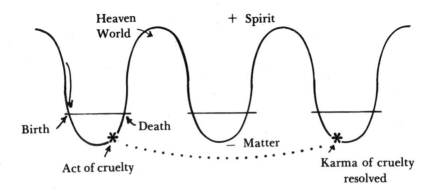

junction, such violent karma is indicated. Mars also indicates karma of fairly recent origin, whereas Saturn indicates karma stemming from causes going back many lives.

Whilst accidents and violence are a characteristic feature of both civilised and uncivilised men, karma is not always implemented with such emphasis. Generally, evil karma will work out through disease. Thus, in Esoteric Healing, such diseases are described under the title of karmic disorders, of which there are many.

KARMIC DISORDERS
1. Mongolism

Mongolism is one of many so-called *karmic disorders* because it is one in which both the Mongol child and the parents are working out karmic factors of a specific kind. The karma of Mongolism itself results from a series of lives in which the mental body has been over-exerted. There has been, in fact, a mental breakdown so frequently that the mental body needs to be rested, even though the physical and astral bodies need at the same time exercising.

Under Such circumstances the soul chooses the body of a Mongol child in which to express itself. In this way, a life is lived — or perhaps even a series of lives — in which the physical and emotional natures are activated in the usual way through reincarnation, but the mental body is rested. There is time for recovery. It is as if the mental body has been put into convalescence or into plaster and is rested, ready for the new life ahead.

The karma of the parents of a Mongol child is fairly average. It relates to the Rays of love and devotion. In previous lives they have been indifferent to the upbringing and nurturing of their children who were perfectly formed. Now they are forced into a life situation in which they are devoted to a child that is malformed, and their devotion is proved by their ability to remain loyal to their offspring despite invidious circumstances.

2. *Rheumatoid Arthritis*

There is karma, however, that embraces more than an individual. Sometimes it embraces a whole subrace. One begins to suspect whether the disease Rheumatoid Arthritis, so prevalent in Britain, is not somehow involved in the karma of this nation.

Rheumatoid arthritis is an inflammatory condition in which the body is invaded by an organism not yet isolated and identified. Subsequent invasions find the body already sensitised by the first. There is a reaction with inflammation of the joints so that there is pain and great difficulty in movement. At its worst, this horrifying disease incarcerates the person in a skeleton that is virtually concrete.

In 1973 I published my first work on Esoteric Healing (Volume One) and maintained there that the organism involved in rheumatoid arthritis is a virus and that it is carried in the dog's saliva and feces. The dog contaminates the parks, bypaths and walks, and people using these areas are liable to infection.

The candidate is usually a person who comes into contact with nature, especially through gardening or taking dogs for walks. They get cuts on their hands and feet through which entry by the virus may occur. The person most vulnerable is the one who has a garden and a dog, who uses a toilet where the hands are washed and, too often, a towel is used again and again so that the virus is passed on through rubbing the towel onto the slightest cuts.

It was not until 1980, however, that British medical doctors came out in force favouring the idea of a virus, though they have yet to identify it. They may find a strong clue, if not in my works, in the fact that the dog population of Britain in relation to the size of the population of humans is the greatest in the world.

What then is the karma of the condition? Not everybody who picks up the virus contracts the disease. Only some. We must search into past lives for the answer.

For many lives, the soul has been unable to expand its consciousness through its vehicle because there has been at the mental and emotional level a concretised outlook; the emotional and mental attitudes have been very crystallised. The personalities used have been insusceptible to argument or suggestion. Life after life, this solidification of the mental and astral bodies has continued progressively. The soul has been unable (indeed, cannot) expand and grow towards greater truth, beauty and goodness because of this barrier.

Consequently, in despair, the soul chooses a life or even a series of lives in which the physical body is susceptible to arthritis. Housed in an arthritic body, virtually immobile, the concreting process is almost complete: the patient is rigid in his thinking, in his feeling and now even in his physical body. This produces eventually, perhaps after several lives, a crisis in which there is a desperate urge to break out from such incarceration, not only at the physical level, but at the emotional and mental as well.

In this way, the soul is freed forever from such a massive encirclement barring the expansion of its consciousness. Even if cure does not come in that traumatic life, the soul is happy enough to lose its physical body. The price has been worth it. *Arthritis will never again play an inhibiting role in this soul's growth.*

This is the way in which karmic diseases work. In the end, they are purifying.

The hope offered here is that even though the physical body may not be cured, the therapist can begin immediately with the reduction of rigidness in the patient's outlook, both mentally and emotionally, knowing full well that the rewards will come if not then, in the lives ahead.

*   *   *

It becomes patent that one life is not enough for the soul to attain its goals. Arthur Shepherd, a Canon of Worchester Cathedral, said :-

> "The apparent inadequacy of a single
> Earth life . . . is given new hope and
> understanding in the realization of the
> process of reincarnation."

It is a pity that the Christian church has not heeded such wise observations as those of Arthur Shepherd or those of the Christians Albert Schweitzer and Leslie Weatherhead, sons of the church who were all reincarnationists.

The North American Red Indian was an example of the influence of the Second Ray. The Indian tribes were lithe, active and colourful with an instinctive love of nature and had tribal institutions which were shattered by the effects of materialism. Their physical bodies were mainly of the Second Ray, with a love of headdress and bodily adornment characteristic of such individuals in our own society who have Second Ray physical vehicles.

The Red Indian was one of the most psychic races which ever lived, a true remnant of Atlantis. Their affinity for the hyperborean continent still shows in their traditional belief in and experience of the "happy hunting grounds" in the sky. The feathered headdress demonstrates that the initiate chiefs knew of the human aura with its layers or interpenetrating bodies.

Spiritual Metamorphosis

What we have been considering so far has been metamorphosis at the spiritual level. All of us know what metamorphosis is for we have seen it in the transition of a caterpillar into the butterfly. We have watched with interest the hatching of a butterfly's egg into a tiny caterpillar which then proceeds to spend its days carving away at every leaf that comes to hand.

As the days pass, it swells and swells to its utmost capacity. Just when we think that it must surely burst, it halts its feasting and begins to spin a cocoon around itself until it disappears within it, shrinking all the time. We then are inclined to believe that it has gone into a state of rest when, in fact, it is now undergoing tremendous changes.

The tiny caterpillar is forming new eyes of a compound nature, growing a proboscis, developing legs and wings, and soon eats its way out of the cocoon's casing of silk to fly off into the orchard as a winged creature, now transformed into a multi-coloured ecstatic being, so different from the earthbound caterpillar characteristic of its early stages of metamorphosis.

The Egyptians were fascinated by the phenomenon of metamorphosis. They lived on the narrow strip of green, cultivated lands that skirted the Nile on either side. Out of the desert came swarms of insects which often devastated their cultivated crops. They never ceased to marvel at the changes that the insects went through and soon identified their own passage from the earth world to the heaven state with those transitions we have mentioned here in insect life. No doubt the fellahine , the peasants of the day, believed that they too would become encased in the equivalent of the cocoon, being perhaps themselves wrapped around in bandages rather than silk at death and, in this way, mummified.

Certainly the Pharaohs were under no illusion about the matter. They believed that they would soon emerge from their sarcophagus after death as a winged being capable of moving into etherial heights.

The Greeks also saw in metamorphosis a deep, inner meaning. Their word for both the butterfly and the soul was *psyche*.

It is a pity that Western man has not had the imaginative resources to conceive of the transition of death as being not unlike that of metamorphosis. The Westerner will grieve over the transition state of death and spend a lot of money on mourning and funerals, instead of focusing his attention on the life that has been freed from its worn out corpse to continue its way through the heaven cycle towards rebirth.

The poem by G. Eustace Owen entitled "A Butterfly" is something that all medical men should read and inwardly digest before they retain people in their worn out physical bodies needlessly.

A Butterfly

A butterfly rested upon a flower,
    Gay was he and light as a flake,
And there he met a caterpillar
    Sobbing as though his heart would
        break;
It hurt the happy butterfly
    To see a caterpillar cry.

Said he, "Whatever is the matter?
    And may I help in any way?"
"I've lost my brother," wept the other,
    "He's been unwell for many a day;
Now I discover, sad to tell,
    He's only a dead and empty shell."

"Unhappy grub, be done with weeping,
    Your sickly brother is not dead;
His body's stronger and no longer
    Crawls like a worm, but flies instead.
He dances through the sunny hours
    And drinks sweet nectar from the
        flowers."

"Away, away deceitful villain,
    Go to the winds where you belong,
I won't be grieving at your leaving,
    So take away your lying tongue.
Am I a foolish slug or snail,
    To swallow such a fairy tale?"

"I'll prove my words, you unbeliever,
    Now listen well, and look at me
I am none other than your brother,
    Alive and well and fancy free.
Soon you'll be with me in the skies
    Among the flirting butterflies."

"Ah!" cried the mournful caterpillar,
    "Tis clear I must be seeing things,
You're only a spectre sipping nectar,
    Flicking your ornamental wings,
And talking nonsense by the yard.
    I will not hear another word."

The butterfly gave up the struggle.
    "I have," he said, "no more to say."
He spread his splendid wings and ascended
    Into the air and flew away.
And while he fluttered far and wide,
    The caterpillar sat and cried.

From *Children's Greater World*

*   *   *   *   *

REINCARNATION

THE CATERPILLAR AND THE BUTTERFLY

45

All the great religions and cultures knew of reincarnation. Some of them glorified it and made it a dominating feature in their way of life; some ignored it as relatively unimportant, and others set out again and again to expunge it as being dangerous or speculative. It greatly depended upon the priests ruling at the time and their inclinations, and whether the doctrine suited their ambitions.

The Old Testament has an esoteric version or commentary, called the Kabbala. Many rabbis today still study the Kabbala as source material and are greatly affected by its erudite and illuminating features. It states that Cain's soul passed into Jethro and that Able's soul passed into Moses.

The peculiar wording of Old Testament tracts that refer to so-and-so being "risen again" refers to the process of rebirth, but those who recorded the Biblical teachings twisted them to suit their own needs, and one does not gather directly from the texts that reincarnation was a central theme of the Old Testament teachings. Scholars will say that the concept was so prevalent that few living in those days felt it necessary to mention it or comment upon it.

The Factor Of Sex

There is no evidence at all that there is any inequality of opportunity being born either as a male or a female. Some ridiculous comments have arisen about alternation of sex in lives. Thus,

> "If a man be niggardly either in a financial or a spiritual regard, giving nothing of his money to the poor or not imparting his knowledge to the ignorant, he shall be punished by transmigration into a woman. . . ."

Generally speaking, we could say that reincarnation in male bodies gives the opportunity to break into new fields of expression at the mental, emotional and physical levels. However, it is equally necessary for the new experiences to be digested, for them to be consolidated in consciousness and for them to be adequately explored. It is in this region of human experience that the role of the female is important. Without this consolidation, usually obtained in female bodies, there can be no further growth.

The male life acts as a frontiersman breaking into new territory, but of equal importance are those lives which establish the frontier firmly, enrich it with culture and art, and stabilise it with family life, etc. There is no question of male chauvinism dominating the doctrine of reincarnation, although there has been this tendency in some interpretations of it.

Margaret Thatcher

One is not able to assess very easily the potential of a national leader in the early days of their accession to the place of power. It is helpful, therefore, when the previous life of such a person is given, for it immediately establishes a precedence which can indicate the potential of the leader, even if that potential is not taken up in this life. At the same time, knowledge of the previous life can point to inherent faults that might emerge in the current life and whose structures are linked to permanent atoms of mental and emotional qualities common to all the lives.

In my book *Esoteric Astrology, Part Three*, I forecast that Margaret Thatcher would win the election, and she did. I wrote there that shortly after her being placed in power, she would become involved in arguments with Europe, and we know that events have shown this.

Britain need never worry about being sold short by Europe under the leadership of Margaret Thatcher, because in the above-mentioned work I indicated that in her previous life she was the Black Prince, the Prince of Wales. He was greatly admired and loved by the English people and was for them, and for most of his life, a favourite. His generalship led England to victory after victory against the French and their allies, both in France and in Spain. Indeed, through his efforts the King of France was captured and brought back to London and a huge ransom was demanded.

We can expect a stubbornness and examples of leadership in dealings with Europe under Margaret Thatcher that we would not be likely to obtain through any other politician.

There is another matter which has karmic significance. At the time of the Black Prince, Europe was swept by plague.

48

It came to England and the population was decimated. Manpower was reduced to such an extent that there were no herdsmen or craftsmen to do the work. Farm animals ran wild untended; ditches and fences could not be repaired; wide areas denuded of population became desolate. England was suddenly lacking in manpower. There just were not enough men availabe to maintain the country's ordinary services, let alone to embark upon new growth or expansion. The Black Prince had great difficulty in obtaining manpower and craftsmen for his army in Europe.

Under karmic circumstances, the exact conditions again apply in England, but in reverse. If someone in a previous life has squandered money or applied it to wrongful ends, he is reborn, under karmic law, into circumstances of poverty whilst being surrounded with wealth which eludes him. Now we have circumstances whereby England (and Europe) is cursed again with an affliction which is karmically in reverse: we have millions unemployed and no work for them. In the earlier karmic events, we had work to be done and no men. This poses a great challenge once more to the soul of Margaret Thatcher . . . namely to find the **best** use for Britain's manpower.

Anyone who has made a study of karma will see the implications here.

Without having any personal political bias, I confidently forecast that the British Prime Minister will lead the country towards greater stability and ascendancy, especially with regard to Europe.

The resoluteness of character, the determination and the finesse of the Black Prince, as well as his predilection for the colour black, show in the nature of the Prime Minister, as it also shows that sex is no barrier to spiritual qualities waiting to be expressed by the soul of any individual.

*   *   *   *   *

Our many lives on Earth teach us the folly of attaching ourselves to things that are transient, that must pass away — places, people and habits.

An ancient sage, no doubt with his tongue in his cheek, commented on this matter :-

> He who feels punctured
> Must once have been a bubble,
> He who feels unarmed
> Must have carried arms,
> He who feels belittled
> Must have been consequential,
> He who feels deprived
> Must have had privilege.

Another lovely commentary is carried in *The Idyll Of The White Lotus* :-

> "Hear me, my brother," he said, "There are three truths which are absolute, and which cannot be lost, but yet may remain silent for lack of speech.
>
> "The soul of man is immortal, and its future is the future of a thing whose growth and splendour has no limit.
>
> "The principle which gives life dwells in us and without us, is undying and eternally beneficent, is not heard or seen, or smelt, but is perceived by the man who desires perception.
>
> "Each man is his own absolute lawgiver, the dispenser of glory or gloom to himself; the decreer of his life, his reward, his punishment.
>
> "These truths, which are as great as is life itself, are as simple as the simplest mind of man. Feed the hungry with them."

The Soul's Purpose

Rudyard Kipling, the poet, once wrote of those who have died :-

> They will come back, come back
>   again as long as the red Earth rolls.
> He never wasted a leaf or a tree.
> Do you think He would squander souls?

And Robert Browning said we have "other tasks in other lives, God willing."

The idea that the soul has a task on Earth to fulfil in each life is implicit in the concept of reincarnation. We are often reminded of the overshadowing influence of the soul in times of crisis when we are sometimes forced to reiterate the profound saying, "Not my will, but Thy will be done, O Lord" (my Father in Heaven, *i.e.*, the soul).

The search for the soul's purpose constitutes the main target for the attention of students of the esoteric sciences. Once this is in the possession of an aspirant, the way becomes clearer, if not easier. Yet, this recognition of the powerful and overshadowing determination of the soul to express itself through its particular life may often show up in every-day events.

In this respect, the following account of how a plane crash altered the life of a sports coach makes interesting reading :-

> An American football coach was onboard a plane with his team, en route to game. The pilot had left the elevator lock on the tail section and tried to abort takeoff, but couldn't. When he tried to land, the right landing gear was unknowingly destroyed. Another landing was attempted, with nearly fatal

results. Eventually, the plane was flown to a Strategic Air Command field for a crash landing on a foamed runway — no casualties.

"That incident had a profound effect on my life," commented the coach. "When you face death four times in one night, you tend to evaluate your priorities, and that night I came to the deep belief that God had a purpose for my life — and not just my life, but everyone."